A Pocket Guide to
Maine
Beaches

D0094578

Cover photograph by Jim Block

ISBN 978-1-60893-044-9

5   4   3   2   1

Down East

Distributed to the trade by National Book Network

A Pocket Guide to
Maine
Beaches

Down East

CONTENTS

Midcoast Maine

Down East Maine

Introduction

For a state famous for its rocky coast, Maine is a beach lover's paradise. From Kittery at the state's southern tip all the way to Portland, long stretches of sand are the rule rather than the exception. But the beaches don't end there—they can be found all the way Down East. There are big barrier beaches and small pocket beaches, beaches of powdery white sand and beaches of singing stones, beaches on the open ocean with thundering breakers and beaches on saltwater rivers with tidal riffles. There are big resort beaches with cotton candy and crowds, arcades and amusement parks, and small wild beaches that few people outside of local residents know. Some of the finest beaches in North America are here, if you believe AOL Travel, Tripadvisor.com, Fodor's, and "America's foremost beach expert," Dr. Beach himself.

Maine is beach country.

This all comes thanks to centuries of fortuitous glaciation and erosion. Ever notice that all of Maine's most famous beaches lie next to rivers? The strands of York sit between the York and Cape Neddick rivers, for example. The Ogunquit River empties just north of Ogunquit Beach. Reid is at the confluence of the Sheepscot and the sea. Popham is on the Kennebec. These river channels were carved by retreating glaciers, and when the big ice continents sloughed off to the south they left massive deposits of minerals behind. Over the centuries, these sands and silts and clays flushed down the big waterways into the Atlantic, which pushed them back up on shore, creating beaches. The finer materials washed away, but the sandy grains collected and stuck.

And across the centuries—from the dawn of civilization, really—people have been flocking to them. There's just something about the big skies, the salt air, the huge expanses of open sea. Whole summer communities have grown up around Maine's long and graceful beaches, from York to Old Orchard to Reid. For many people who flock north each year, the sun and sand and surf are the very stuff of a Maine vacation. They come to swim and sunbathe; spread out their blankets and park their chairs, to dig their toes into warm sand, build sandcastles, and learn how to surf. It's really no surprise that southern Maine is the most visited region of Vacationland—that's where most of the beaches are.

Whatever beach experience you want—big and boisterous, quiet and serene, full of body surfing or simply a romantic stroll—you can find it in Maine.

1

KITTERY

Seapoint and Crescent Beaches

Off Route 103. Take Seapoint Road from Thaxter Road and look for the signs.

Latitude: 43.0879

Longitude: -70.6623

Kittery is known more for out*lets* than for the out*doors*—among all the towns of southern Maine, it is probably the least associated with beaches. But it does indeed have several strands. The two that are arguably the most popular are Seapoint and Crescent, which flank Seapoint, a small peninsula between Gerrish Island and Brave Boat Harbor in Kittery Point. Both of them are pretty small compared to others up the road in York and Ogunquit and Wells—they're in the 600-yard range—but they don't tend to get as busy as the larger beaches do, either. You can usually find a place to spread out without too much difficulty.

What is hard, though, is parking. There's a lot five minutes

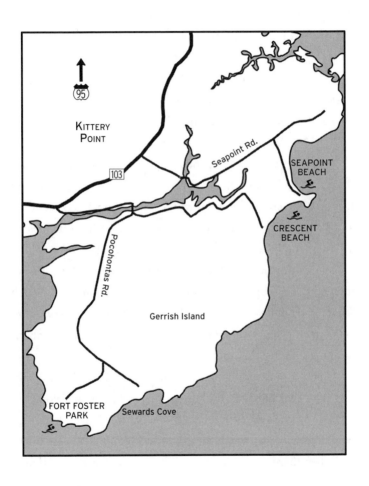

away, but it's for town residents only and you have to have a Kittery solid waste sticker or face a $500 fine if you park there out of season. The lots are closed to non-residents from May 15 to September 30—basically prime beach season. The good news is that you can pose as a Kittery town resident by buying a sticker; the bad news is that there are only one hundred available each season, on a first-come basis, and they cost $125.

The locals are very protective of this pair of beaches.

Are they worth it? Depends on your interest. These are not the finest sands, but rather composed of course gray grains. And they're often covered in tidal wrack—huge bunches of seaweed and kelp—that attracts nasty green-eyed flies. If your idea of a day at the beach is sunbathing, body surfing, and napping on soft sand, neither of these is the place for you. But if you're there to swim, walk, and explore, then you're in business. Watch where you put down your towel, though, as this is a very popular place for dog lovers, and they're not always diligent about cleaning up after their pets.

Right in the middle of Seapoint Beach is a tumble of rocks in a jetty that kids will find interesting to climb, and you pass through sections of the Rachel Carson National Wildlife Refuge on your way in, so watch for egrets and other interesting birds. And then there are the views out to the sea. The open Atlantic spreads out before you, and it's magnificent. The beach is long and gradual and the surf tends to be smaller than at many other beaches, with waves that break long before they get to the sands and never get much above shin level on a normal day. Which makes it great for kids.

Projecting out into the Atlantic between Seapoint and Crescent is the grassy peninsula known as Seapoint. Shaped like the head of a hammer, it's owned by the Kittery Land Trust, which is part of the Maine Land Trust Network. (It was donated by a local family in honor of Rosamond Thaxter, who was the granddaughter of Celia Thaxter and wrote a biography of the famed poet entitled *Sandpiper*.) Dunes, marshes, and rocks prevail here and it's very popular among area cyclists and dog walkers. There are nice views out to Nubble Light and the Isles of Shoals.

Crescent Beach sits on the north side of this peninsula, and it's much like Seapoint, though it tends to be rockier. Some cobbles can be as big as a fist—and at high tide the beach all but vanishes.

There are no facilities to speak of at either beach, no bathhouses or snack bars. And there are no lifeguards to watch over you. So be careful out in the surf. Kids like to party here at night, too, so keep that in mind when making your plans.

No fee.

OTHER BEACHES IN KITTERY

Fort Foster Park
Pocahontas Road, 207-439-2182
Latitude: 43.0679
Longitude: -70.6884

An old bastion on Gerrish Island, Fort Foster was built in 1872 to protect the entrance to Portsmouth Harbor. And the place remained active right up through World War II, when a net was strung across the water to Portsmouth in the hopes of snagging U-Boats. Today, it's still active—with day-trippers and summer swimmers.

There's more grass than sand at this southern Maine beach, but you can find a few small arcs on which to place your towel at the ninety-acre town park. The waves are gentle, there are shallows for the kids, and there's a playground and picnic tables for after your dip. The views out on the Piscataqua and across to Whaleback Light are fine.

Open 10 A.M. to 8 P.M., Memorial Day through Labor Day. Admission is $10 per car, $5 per person if walking or biking in.

2

YORK

Harbor Beach

Route 1A, 207-363-1040
Latitude: 43.1329
Longitude: -70.6377

Harbor Beach is one of the more petite strands in southern Maine, and there's something quite cute about it. A crescent smile of sand between a residential headland and the hulking Stage Neck Inn, the beach is a little stunner staring out into York Harbor. But its diminutive size makes it all the more difficult to get onto. Don't expect to find any parking. You might want to rent a bike or take a cab—it's that congested here. If you're lucky you can find a spot on the street across from the York Harbor Inn, but in the summer these spaces are about as fleeting as an empty tollbooth on the turnpike the Friday before a holiday weekend.

With gentle surf and pebbly sands, this small cul-de-sac is a fine swimmers beach. At high tide there's not much sand left

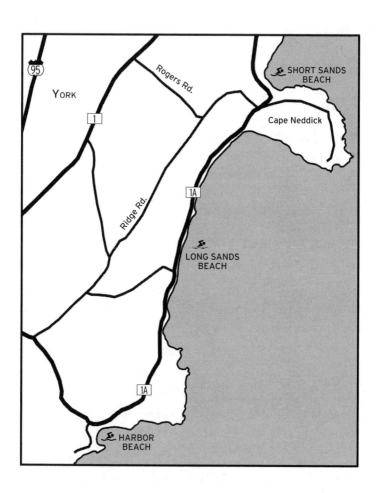

between the water and the cobbles at the head of the beach, but when the tide is out there's enough sand to get a quick jog in before you're up to your knees. The waves are fairly gentle here, as the sands are gradual, and a light ripple is more common than any sort of breakers. Because of its small size, competition for places to put your umbrella or your towel is fairly vigorous.

Nearby, though, there is a lot to do. Hartley Mason Park, a small green with shade trees and benches, sits on a hill overlooking the beach. York's famous Cliff Path, a thrilling walkway that, just as its name suggests, follows the edge of the headland lofting up over the harbor. You walk right through the backyards of some of the area's finest summer homes. A few neat shops line the streets of York Harbor, and there is some nice dining at the York Harbor Inn.

A few years back, Harbor Beach was given a facelift, with a new parking lot and new restrooms, so there are some facilities. Lifeguards are on duty from the end of June through Labor Day.

No fee.

Long Sands and Short Sands Beaches

Route 1A, 207-363-1040

Long Sands:

Latitude: 43.1549

Longitude: -70.6223

Short Sands:

Latitude: 43.1747

Longitude: -70.6071

One of the great resort beaches of southern Maine, Long Sands is right in the thick of things, sitting off Route 1A between York Harbor and York Beach. On one side of the old Atlantic Highway are miles of hotels and motels and on the other side is the beach—Long Sands is indeed long. The beach extends more than a mile and a half, paralleling the road. Fairly fine grained, the sand seems to go on forever.

Because this beach is so lengthy there is more room to spread out than on some of Maine's other beaches. Of course, it's right down the road from all the amusements of York Beach, in an area overrun every summer by hordes of tourists, so it's not exactly wide open. But you can usually find a place to spread your blanket without elbowing the person next to you or cutting across someone's towel every time you want to dip your toes in.

Be careful where you set up, though, because if you don't pay mind to the tides you might wake up from your nap neck deep in the cold Atlantic. The beach all but disappears at high tide, the water coming almost up to the seawall at sand's end. Better to bring a chair, actually, than a towel or blanket because the sand tends to stay damp, and unless it's plastic lined, your spread will get wet.

Because it is inundated twice daily, the beach is on the firm side, which makes it ideal for volleyball, beach soccer, Frisbee, jogging, and other sports. Long Sands is also one of the few Maine beaches with a designated surfing area. There is a whole community of surfers who hang out and hang-ten here—Grain Surfboards, which builds handmade surfboards of local sustainable wood, is based in York (grainsurfboards.com). Boogie boards, banned on so many Down East beaches, are also welcome. Surfs up, indeed.

The beach is great for children, especially when the tide is on the way out. When it's at its lowest, the tide exposes about a half mile of sand, sloping gradually, so kids can play and splash and make sandcastles without parents worrying too much about them. (Watch those tides, though.) There are also some great tide pools for exploring among the rocks. Crabs, starfish, periwinkles, sand dollars—all the tide-pool favorites—can be found.

Backing up to the beach are hundreds of metered parking spots, but they go very fast on nice days. Snack shacks can be found all over and it's clean and pleasant for such a popular spot. Lifeguards are on duty in July and August, and there are both bathhouses and restrooms.

Cross Cape Neddick, a residential peninsula, and you'll arrive at Short Sands Beach, the little sibling of Long Sands. The sand here is so short, in fact, that it disappears altogether when the tide comes all the way in. The cramped space makes for a tight fit in high summer—the beach can get very crowded with chairs and towels and bodies. On a hot August weekend they can cover every available space, including the rocks.

Of course, the beach is only one of the amusements in York. The famous Goldenrod candy store is just a short walk away. As are York's Wild Kingdom petting zoo, the Fun-O-Rama arcade, basketball courts, t-shirt shops, fried-food stands, and all the other trappings of a beach resort. You can find everything from saltwater taffy to Hawaiian ice to ice cream to lobster ten different ways, all within an easy stroll.

Like so many of Maine's most spectacular public places, Short Sands was donated by generous benefactors. Often these gifts—imagine what this southern Maine beach is worth today— go unnoticed. Ellis Park, as this area is sometimes known, was saved in perpetuity for all to enjoy in August of 1887, a present to the people of the area from the Ellis, Moseley, and Garmon families. Talk about foresight. That was long before development pressure put the squeeze on the state's highly desirable—and relatively rare—stretches of beachfront, and realtors began to sell the adjacent land for all it was worth. Those generous families saw their share of tourists—the trolleys began to run in 1897—but they couldn't have imagined what it would look like today. On sweltering August weekends, the public certainly puts this lovely gift of sand to good use.

Long and Short Sands Beaches have metered parking off Route 1A—stuff your swim shorts with quarters (but remember to take them out before you get in the water). Cops patrol these spaces on bikes with ticket books in hand. There are also parking lots here and there that charge $5–$10 a day. A better bet might be to park elsewhere and hop the York Trolley, which visits the beaches every half hour between 10 A.M. and 10:15 P.M. during the summer.

3

OGUNQUIT

Ogunquit Beach
Beach Street, 207-646-2939
Latitude: 43.2554
Longitude: -70.5905

In 1888 some enterprising locals built a bridge across the Ogunquit River—and that was it. Beachgoers have been swarming across to the beach on the far side for more than a century. In fact, people have been visiting this stretch of coast all along—the Abenaki term *ogunquit* means "beautiful place by the sea," and they came here to frolic in the sand. On a hot summer day it seems the whole world is visiting these three miles of pristine white sand.

It's easy to understand why.

Ogunquit is a beach-lover's beach. Long and powdery, it has arguably the finest white sand in Maine—perhaps even in New England. There are hardly any rocks and little or no seaweed.

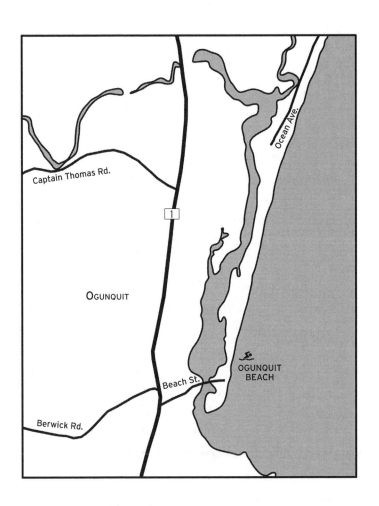

Captain Thomas Rd.

1

OGUNQUIT

Ocean Ave.

OGUNQUIT
BEACH

Beach St.

Berwick Rd.

The tidal wrack is minimal. There are just miles of soft sand, deep and wide.

This is an exceptional example of a barrier-spit beach, where a long arm of land sits between the open sea and a lagoon, and it is a breathtaking place. In this case, the Ogunquit River creates an estuary that naturally separates the village from the beach. Turn your back to the town, with its houses and hotels and commercial development, and face out to the Atlantic—all you can see are miles of beach, rolling breakers, and the open sea.

With miles of space, delicate sand, and breakers to play in, Ogunquit Beach is perfect for almost any beach activity. Swimming, surfing, walking and jogging, building castles, simply sunbathing—you name it, the place is ideal. (And you can swim with confidence here—the lifeguards train four times a week and have consistently placed high in the Northern New England Lifesaving Championships.) Kids love to fish off the Footbridge and splash in the basin created by the river, where the water is warmer. It is a romantic place where lovers stroll; sandcastle competitions heat up in July; and a host of events, from fireworks to dances, take place here during the summer.

Everything you might forget for a day at the beach—food, sunscreen, umbrella, chair, boogie board, bocce set—can be rented at Ogunquit Beach 'n' Sport (68 Shore Road, 207-351-

7840, ogtbeachnsport.com). Concessions are limited to the parking lots, but you can get some delicious lunch foods at the stands there.

Ogunquit Beach is extraordinarily popular. On a hot summer day, the beach can get crowded—and fast—especially at high tide. The gentle slope, which is great for kids and strollers, becomes something of a problem when the tide comes in. The surf flows very high up onto the sands, pushing all the people back with it. At low tide there can be 200 yards of open space, but when the water returns, space comes at a real premium and you see beachgoers spilling right off the beach onto the side-walks. Everyone wants a piece of it.

These sorts of pressures have been a concern here ever since the bridge was built, and the people of Ogunquit have made a real effort to preserve the sanctity of their beach. Back in the day, forward-thinking citizens concerned that the beach would fall to commercial development launched a petition drive. They turned their signatures in to the Maine Legislature, asking that the area on the other side of the Ogunquit River be sold to the town. And amazingly they succeeded. In 1938, they bought the beach for $45,000 and designated the whole area as a park.

This has done wonders for the dunes, which were almost trampled to death by foot traffic. All those excited beachgoers walking through the rare beach grass loosened the dunes and they began to crumble. Sand blew off in windstorms or washed into the estuary, sullying the water quality. (The Patriot's Day storm in April 2007 took a massive toll here, eroding huge sections of beach and dunes. Thanks to a cooperative effort between FEMA, the Town of Ogunquit, and a host of state agencies, the dunes have been once again restored and the charismatic little piping plovers that love them are back.)

Today the beach is well looked after—access is limited to just three entry points and most of the commercial activity of the town is kept at bay. There are three main sections—the large stretch accessed from town known as plain old Ogunquit Beach; Footbridge Beach in the middle; and Moody Beach up by Wells.

Anyone planning a visit to Ogunquit Beach would be wise to schedule a bit of time to walk the Marginal Way, a 1.25-mile seaside pedestrian path linking the beach area with Perkins Cove. Fronting a jaw-dropping panorama and hugging the side of a cliff the whole way, this paved walkway is a local favorite.

Facilities are impressive, with restrooms and changing areas and outdoor showers at several points. Parking is $20–$25, depending upon where you go. Unless you arrive early, forget about parking anywhere nearby—best to take the trolley in, which makes trips to both ends of the beach three or four times an hour.

4

WELLS

Wells Beach

Webhannet Drive/Atlantic Avenue, 207-646-2451

Latitude: 43.3029

Longitude: -70.5659

Set between Ogunquit to its south and Kennebunk to its north, the town of Wells is, essentially, one long beach. From Moody Beach at the end of Ogunquit to the Webhannet River at the northern end of town, the community's coastline is broken up into a bunch of strands—Moody, Drakes, Laudholm, and Crescent beaches—that stretch for more than five miles from one end of town to the other. And then there's the namesake beach—by far the biggest and most popular, 4,000 feet of fine sand fronting the open sea, next stop France.

The town of Wells proper is separated from the Atlantic by Webhannet Marsh and the Webhannet River, which create a peninsula that stretches out as a protective barrier. On the sea

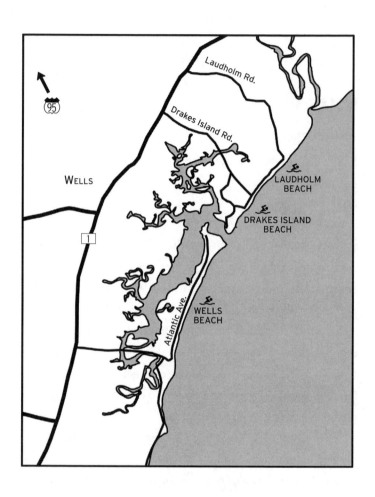

side of this long, skinny finger is the beach, backed by a cement wall; on the other is a line of condos and cottages that look out across the street at the limitless blue expanse and pour people onto the sand all day long. There is public access on almost every block with little paths wandering out onto its warm sand. Good luck finding parking, though.

Near the midpoint of this sprawling beach is the village of Wells Beach, where there are shops, restaurants, an arcade, snackbars—all of those commercial places that seem to sprout up alongside beaches. You can find all of the necessities here.

The beach is long enough and everything is so spread out that if you can find a place to park you're practically guaranteed your own wide swath of beach. Lifeguards keep careful watch over the goings on. (In 2002 the beach was even closed because of repeated sightings of some big sharks.) Many people like to jog on the sand, but the beach is so big you aren't likely to trip over one another.

Like its sibling to the south in Ogunquit, Wells Beach has been a favorite recreational destination for hundreds of years. The natives called the area *Webhannet*—"at the clear stream"— for the vast marshes here. And they like to gathered at the spot for bonfires and swimming. When the English moved in, the region was part of the Gorges Grant, given to Sir Ferdinando

Gorges by the Plymouth Company in 1622, and it became the third incorporated community in Maine in 1653. At the time, Wells included all of Ogunquit and the Kennebunks.

The settlers seemed more concerned about the hay of Webhannet Marsh than the beach itself. This sea straw was extremely important to early settlers to feed their animals (so much so that in 1757, Massachusetts—to which the Province of Maine belonged—passed a law outlawing the trampling of the dunes by livestock). Today the marsh is valued most by seabirds. Wells is the headquarters of the Rachel Carson National Wildlife Refuge—a favorite of our avian friends—and a great deal of acreage is preserved here. Dozens of bird species have been spotted in and around the refuge.

The arrival of passenger trains to the coast in the late nineteenth century put Wells on the map as an oceanside resort and it's been so ever since. And once again you can ride the rails here—Wells has a stop on Amtrak's Downeaster Line (amtrakdowneaster.com).

Parking is $15 a day or $75 for ten days at a handful of lots: Mile Road (at the end of Mile Road), Eastern Shore (at the end of Atlantic Avenue), Gross (off Drakes Island Road), and Drakes Island (at the end of the Drakes Island Road). Parking passes can be purchased at a lot or at the town hall.

OTHER BEACHES IN WELLS

Drakes Island and Laudholm Beaches

Drakes Island Road, 207-646-2451

Latitude: 43.3242

Longitude: -70.5509

The jetty that ends Wells Beach marks the start of Drakes Island Beach, which stretches north and joins with Laudholm Beach. This pair of beaches sprawls for about a half mile and they are one of the longest strands in a town famous for them. It's a white-sand beach with nice wave action to play in, and it's typically a little quieter than the more touristed Wells Beach (though you may not notice on a hot day in August).

Facilities here are limited, though there are lifeguards, restrooms, and parking. But that makes a day here all the more special. The views out to the open sea are spectacular. Laudholm Beach is part of the Wells National Estuarine Research Reserve, so when you've had enough splashing and swimming you can check out this natural wonderland. Watch for the comical packs of plovers and hit the trails that thread through the reserve.

5

THE KENNEBUNKS

Kennebunk Beach

Beach Avenue, off Routes 9 and 35, Kennebunk, 207-967-0857
Latitude: 43.3444
Longitude: -70.5022

Kennebunk Beach isn't really a beach. It's a mile of sand divided into three distinct sections—Mother's, Middle, and Gooch's beaches—all set off Beach Avenue on the seaside of a busy, heavily developed residential area. These stretches of beach are connected by a sidewalk that runs along the road behind them—a stroll along this pedestrian highway is the highlight of many a vacation—and together they meld into one great beach that is among the treasures of southern Maine. (A fine place to be on the Fourth of July, too, when fireworks explode colorfully overhead.)

Curled up south of Lord's Point is Mother's Beach, the smallest of the Kennebunk beaches at about 750 feet long. As its name suggests, this short sandy strip has long been a favored destination

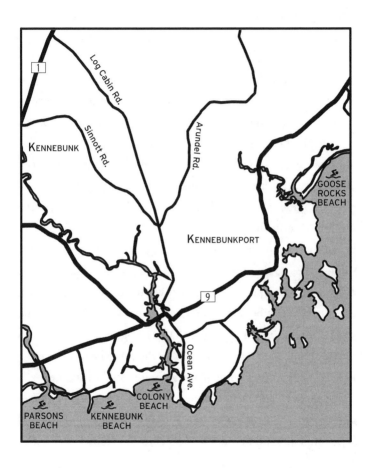

of families. It's tucked into a small, sheltered cove, which protects it from big swells, and the slope to the sea is gradual and easy for small feet. When the tide recedes it leaves behind many tide pools to explore. And right on the sand is a playground. Lifeguards maintain a daily vigil in summer, which should please any mother at Mother's Beach. There are restrooms but no concessions or other facilities. For those you can walk the short distance up Beach Avenue to the Lower Village. Parking is by permit only.

North of Mother's Beach is the aptly named Middle Beach—about a quarter mile of dark sand shaped like a widow's peak, and backed by a seawall. This beach is more pebbly, not so pleasant under towels, so bring a beach chair. When the waves wash back out, the stones make a pleasant clatter. This isn't a beach for running barefoot or sleeping on a blanket or building sandcastles, but more for exploring tide pools and enjoying the ocean vistas. People have been known to stroll on Middle, and the breakers can be surfed on a good day. When the tide comes in, the beach is much narrower than its neighbors, which would crowd things if it were as popular as the other beaches in town. But since it isn't, it's a fine place to swim in relative quiet.

And just around the corner is Gooch's Beach. Sometimes referred to as Kennebunk Beach, it is the most popular stretch in town. The sand at Gooch's stretches for 3,300 feet between

Narragansett Point and the Kennebunk River, which empties into the sea at the north end. The beach makes a long, wide arc, and the sands are fine. This is the beach to visit for all the traditional fun—bodysurfing, sunning, people watching, castle building, long hand-holding walks, lazy naps on the sand. Many people like to walk to the jetty at the mouth of the river to watch the endless to and fro of boats. When the tide is really cresting here it can push very high up the beach, again constraining the space. Gooch's has lifeguards and restrooms.

Parking at Mother's, Middle, and Gooch's beach is by permit only. Passes can be purchased by the day ($5), week ($15), or the season ($30) at the town office, the police station, and the chamber of commerce. Another idea is to park in the public lots at Grove Street or the Lower Village (behind the fire station) and catch the shuttle (a day pass is $3).

Goose Rocks Beach

Kings Highway, Kennebunkport, 207-967-0857
Latitude: 43.4007
Longitude: -70.4078

Sprawling for more than two miles, Goose Rocks Beach is one of the most unspoiled and picturesque of all Maine's beaches.

AOL Travel has called Kennebunkport one of "America's Best Beach Towns," and since it's really the only beach in town, Goose Rocks has to be what they're talking about.

Paralleling Kings Highway in Kennebunkport, "GRB" as the locals call it, stares out at the small archipelago of islands from which it takes its name. These craggy rocks poke up into Goosefair Bay, and geese are said to use them as waypoints on their migrations. Along with Timber Island, they protect the beach from the full brunt of the sea, making it a great family destination. The breakers are on the small side and the slope is very gradual. Kids love the place.

Everybody, it seems, loves Goose Rocks. The beach has a reputation for being clean, relatively quiet, and not over-crowded thanks to limited parking and a lack of facilities. (You have to walk up to the general store to find a bathroom.) It's not a beer-and-boom-box sort of beach, but rather the kind where grandparents take the kids for the day, couples stroll hand in hand, and sandcastles are serious business. The flat and wide nature of the beach makes it ideal for volley-ball, soccer, Frisbee, or for just about any physical activity. And there's always enough room that you won't be bothering anyone else if you're considerate.

Though this beach is peaceful, the adventurous can find

excitement by walking to the northeast end and wading across the channel out to the isles there. Caution is in order, of course—be careful of the currents and mindful of the tides or you'll get stranded.

Just like at so many other waterfront spots in Maine, access has become an issue at GRB. Ownership of this spectacular acreage is in question, and twenty-four families with waterfront deeds have sued the town to limit public use. Kennebunkport has been actively working to keep it open, trotting out deeds dating back to the seventeenth century. Visitors who want to be able to swim here in the future would be wise to be as low impact and courteous as possible. Dogs are welcome before 8 A.M. and after 6 P.M.

Parking is very limited and permits are required. (There's a very active bike-mounted police patrol here.) Passes can be purchased by the day ($12) or by the week ($50) at the police station, the Kennebunkport Town Office, the Kennebunk/Kennebunkport Chamber of Commerce, or the Goose Rocks General Store.

OTHER BEACHES IN THE KENNEBUNKS

Colony Beach

Ocean Avenue, Kennebunkport, 207-967-0857
Latitude: 43.3412
Longitude: -70.4673

Also known as Arundel Beach, this is a blink-and-you-miss-it beach right across the street from the famous Colony Hotel at the mouth of the Kennebunk River. Guests at the grand hotel are frequent visitors to the 150 feet of sand and pebbles at this tiny beach. It's a cute spot, curled up and protected, and offers some nice views, too. And the swimming is good as well.

What you won't find here are any amenities. It's more of a secret getaway than what people think of when they imagine a southern Maine beach. There are no lifeguards, no concession stands, no umbrella rentals, no restrooms—you get the idea. There is a small gravel parking area, but it fills fast in summer. The Parson's Way shore path begins here, and it's a pleasant stroll along the edge of the sea.

No fee.

Parsons Beach

Parsons Beach Road, Kennebunk
Latitude: 43.3437
Longitude: -70.5184

The quietest of beaches in the Kennebunks, Parsons is private, but the public is allowed to use it in limited fashion. No parties, no bonfires, no surfing, no motorized vehicles, no trampling the rare beach grass or removing found objects—in short, be respectful.

At the outlet of the Mousam River, the beach is open and unspoiled, backed by marshes, framed by dunes, with a slight hill descending to the sand. The Rachel Carson National Wildlife Refuge protects much of the estuarine land along the shore of the river and behind the beach, giving the place a wild and remote atmosphere.

Because it's relatively secluded, this was once a favorite place for topless sunbathing. Parking is very limited. Many people like to rent bikes in town and pedal over.

No fee.

6

SACO

Ferry Beach State Park
95 Bayview Road, 207-283-0067
Latitude: 43.4768
Longitude: -70.3844

Ferry Beach State Park is not to be confused with Ferry Beach. The state park is the 1,700-yard white sand strand run by the State of Maine in Saco. The other is a small neighborhood crescent on a river in exclusive Prouts Neck. Same name—ferries must have been busy along the south coast at one time—but very different places.

Ferry Beach State Park sits between Camp Ellis to the south and Old Orchard to the north, on the site of the old ferry across the Saco River. And it's something to behold. Maine owns 117 acres here, prime real estate, and you can almost forget you're in heavily developed southern Maine when you wander through its woods on the 1.7-mile network of board-walked trails. Indeed,

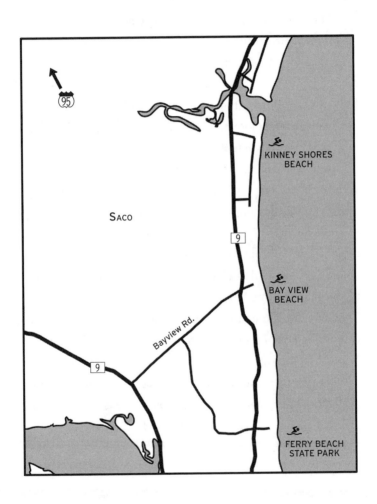

the park is full of natural wonders, not the least of which is a stand of tupelo trees, swamp-dwelling plants that are very rare at this northern latitude.

Of course, most people who visit this Saco staple come for the sand, and the beach here is beautiful. Wide, open, fine, and backed up by dunes, it is made for beach lovers. It tends to be much quieter and more private than the strands of Old Orchard, which sit just up Route 9.

Bring a picnic and some comfortable walking shoes with your towel and tanning lotion and make a day of it. Don't forget to sign up for the ranger-led programs if you really want to get to know the place. You'll learn a host of interesting facts, about the old railroad that used to traverse the dunes transporting people between Old Orchard and Camp Ellis or about some of the more interesting flora and fauna.

Changing rooms and bathrooms are available, and parking is typically less of a problem than it is at many other southern Maine beaches.

Day-use fees are $4 for adult Maine residents, $6 non-resident; Maine seniors are free, non-resident seniors are $2; children ages 5–11 are $1, under 5 are free.

OTHER BEACHES IN SACO

Bay View Beach

Route 9, 207-283-3139

Latitude: 43.4853

Longitude: -70.3854

Part of the huge, seven-mile swath of sand that curves from Camp Ellis in Saco to Pine Point in Scarborough, this small city-run beach is next door to Ferry Beach State Park and Kinney Shores Beach. The parking area sits just off Route 9, and there are restrooms. Park your car (parking is limited), walk past the grass and dunes, find a place on the sand, and take in the magnificent views of Saco Bay. Lifeguards are on duty from late June to mid-August.

Kinney Shores Beach

Route 9, 207-283-3139

Latitude: 43.4931

Longitude -70.3881

Sandwiched between Bay View Beach and Ocean Park, this city-run beach is yet another way to get onto the sands of Saco

Bay. A barrier spit, the beach protects Goosefare Brook and its wetlands, which sit behind a dense residential area of summer homes. Because of all the private development, it can be very hard to find parking. And, another bummer, there are no public restrooms.

Like so many other coastal areas in this part of Maine, it was hammered by the Patriot's Day Storm in 2007 and suffered considerable erosion. Much of the damage, though, has been restored.

Lifeguards are on duty from late June to mid August.

7

OLD ORCHARD BEACH

Old Orchard Beach
Beach Street, 207-934-2500
Latitude: 43.5165
Longitude: -70.3721

On a hot August day, Old Orchard Beach becomes the largest town in Maine. As many as 100,000 revelers might line up to enjoy its seven miles of sand—and all the raucous entertainments that spin and whirl around them. This is the beach of beaches in the state, the center of beach culture, the Coney Island, the Jersey Shore, the Ocean City. If you like your beaches backed up to arcades, fried-food stands, souvenir shops, pizza joints, and amusement park rides, this is the place for you.

The beach stretches all the way from Saco to Scarborough—it was created by the outpouring of sand from the Saco and Scarborough rivers. In the middle of everything—both literally and figuratively—is the Pier, a 500-foot-long jetty that houses

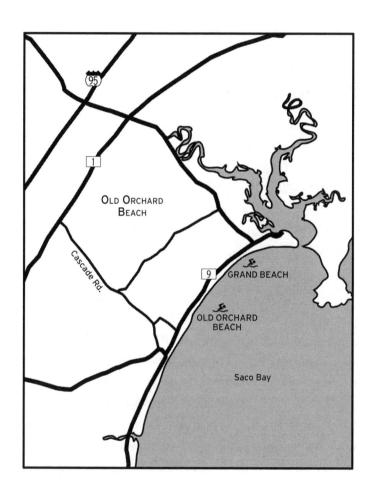

restaurants, bars, and shops and serves as a focal point around which all the other establishments revolve. Need a painted-on or real tattoo, braided hair, or a souvenir t-shirt? This is where you would begin looking. Pier french fries are sublime. (Parking anywhere near here is expensive—a quarter for seven minutes at the meters.)

New England's only beachfront amusement park, Palace Playland, is right nearby. Here kids of all ages find roller coasters, carousels, a Ferris wheel, funhouse, and all kinds of other rides for which Mainers usually have to await the arrival of a state fair.

It's really astonishing the amount of things to do here beyond the beach. Parasailing? Check. Championship mini golf? Check. Kayak rental? Check. Deepwater fishing? Check. Horseback riding? Check. Balloon rides? Check. The list goes on and on and on.

Old Orchard Beach has been this way for hundreds of years. Ages ago, sailors along the Maine coast would navigate using the apple orchard that stood above seven long miles of beach south of the Scarborough River. They called the place Old Orchard. The first settler to stick his toes in the sand here was probably Thomas Rogers, who set down roots in "Garden by the Sea," as he called the area, in 1657. His house was eventually burned by angry Abenakis.

In 1820 the first entrepreneur opened an inn here, recognizing the potential of the beach as a getaway. Rail service in the 1850s brought all kinds of tourists to that hostelry—and all the boarding houses and hotels that followed. Old Orchard Beach was growing in popularity among not just Mainers but also Bostonians and residents of New Hampshire. And when the Grand Trunk Railroad opened in 1853, connecting the beach to Montreal, French-Canadians started to make annual pilgrimages—a trend that has continued unabated ever since.

The year 1898 brought the first pier, a steel structure that stretched 1,770 feet out into the water. A November storm that year wiped it out, and a new one was built. The first amusement park opened in 1902 with a merry-go-round, games of chance, rollerskating, and refreshments. Kids hopped aboard—and their parents hopped in the clubs at night. During the 1920s, they danced to Duke Ellington and Guy Lombardo and played games at the Pier Casino. After Charles Lindbergh made his momentous flight across the Atlantic in 1927, other aviators attempted to follow suit and a host of them used the packed sands of Old Orchard Beach as their runway.

The beach buzzed all through the twentieth century. The Pier was wrecked again by a massive storm in 1978, and the current version was built in 1980. The honky-tonk vibe of Old

Orchard Beach developed over the years and threatened to spill over into unlawfulness. In the 1980s and 90s a certain seedy cast fell over the beach.

But in the early 2000s there was a real effort to renew and revitalize—to make Old Orchard Beach again a welcoming place for families. The beach and the downtown were spiffed up, landscaping was put in, noise ordinances were passed, and a new slogan was adopted, "It's a Shore Thing."

Once again, though, it's starting to look a little shabby.

Parking can be found in several commercial and municipal lots or in metered spots on the street. Fees vary, depending upon distance from the beach and who owns the lot. Otherwise, facilities at Old Orchard Beach are readily available.

OTHER BEACHES IN OLD ORCHARD BEACH

Grand Beach
Route 9 (East Grand Avenue)
Latitude: 43.5325
Longitude: -70.3596

This is the beach where the sands of York County flow into those of Greater Portland. At the end of Old Orchard Beach, this 2,500-yard stretch of sand is more an extension of the state's most famous beach than a destination in its own right. Still, it offers great swimming, some grand views of the tony neighborhood of Prout's Neck, and there's a rocky breakwater here that people like to fish from.

Facilities include a snack bar, bathhouse, and some parking in a very residential area.

8

SCARBOROUGH

Scarborough Beach State Park

418 Black Point Road, 207-883-2416
Latitude: 43.5470
Longitude: -70.3053

Scarborough Beach is a curious thing. It's a state park run by a private corporation; a full-service beach far from Route 1 and its boardwalks and t-shirt and snack shops; and a fantastic public place in the most exclusive of neighborhoods. There isn't another beach quite like it in Maine.

Of course, what matters on a hot day are the sand and the surf, and this half-mile beach has some of the finest around. The sand is white and the breakers come in booming. The beach faces the open Atlantic from the east, or ocean, side of Prout's Neck. (It used to be you wouldn't venture here unless you had the correct last name or were visiting someone who did—and you wouldn't even think about parking.) On the other side of

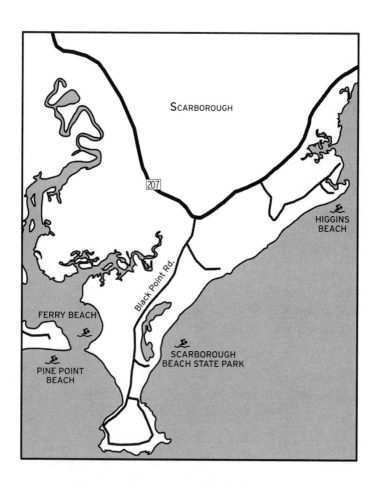

this neck are Ferry and Western beaches, neighborhood strands you can walk to if you want a smaller, quieter experience.

Why bother, though, when you have all this in front of you? Scarborough Beach has everything a beachgoer could want, and then some. The sand is long with plenty of room to spread out and the water is remarkably warm—high 60s. The sand is comfortable enough for napping or jogging, and the surf is great for boogie-boarding and even surfing. (Boogie boards can be rented for $5; surfing requires a permit.) The "Shack" provides drinks and all kinds of light fare, from pizza to wraps, and even rents umbrellas and chairs. Lifeguards are on duty in the peak season (June 10–Labor Day). And there are changing rooms, too.

Parking is available for about four hundred cars, including at the off-site spaces. But as many as a thousand people can show up on a hot Saturday, so plan to get there early. Fees are $4.50 for adult Maine residents, $6.50 for non-residents; kids are $2, and seniors are free; non-resident seniors are $2. Vehicle passes allowing access to three parks can be purchased for $70.

OTHER BEACHES IN SCARBOROUGH

Pine Point Beach

Avenue 5, off King Street, 207-730-4000

Latitude: 43.5406

Longitude: -70.3367

This is the best beach in Maine—according to the readers of the *Portland Press Herald.* (Neighbor Higgins Beach came in a close second.) Set on the peninsula where the Scarborough River meets the sea—essentially the entrance to the great Scarborough Marsh— Pine Point is a sprawling beach that extends for four miles.

Run by the town of Scarborough, the beach is ideal for any sort of sun, sand, and surf activities. The sand is fine and the beach is wide even at high tide. The approach is gradual and there is some nice wave action for playing in the breakers. Surfing is allowed.

The town takes good care of the beach, keeping it clean and raking it weekly. Full facilities here include public restrooms, showers, and a concession stand, but there are no lifeguards.

Parking off Avenue 5, which is off King Street, is just $10. Seasonal passes can be purchased at the town municipal building for a mere $20.

Ferry Beach

Off Route 207, 207-730-4000
Latitude: 43.5437
Longitude: -70.3217

Not to be confused with the much more popular Ferry Beach State Park in Saco, this Ferry Beach is a local favorite that fronts the Scarborough River and marsh. This places it on the opposite side of the Prout's Neck peninsula from Scarborough Beach and makes it the rare saltwater beach that actually faces west. It's a neat inlet with fine sand that follows the contours of the river, and the beach feels riverine, with a boathouse on one end and actual lobsterboats moored in the channel. The view across the way is of Pine Point, a seasonal Scarborough enclave. Walk far enough to the south at Ferry and you'll find yourself on the adjacent Western Beach. Between the two of them, there are about 1,700 yards of fine sand. Swimming is safer at Western because of the deep drop-off and current of the river channel at Ferry.

Access is off Route 207 (Black Point Road)—look for signs. Parking is $10 per car in the hundred or so sites of the town-run lot and seasonal passes can be had for $20. There are restrooms and showers, too. Get there early to get a spot, and don't even think of parking anywhere near heavily policed Prout's Neck, perhaps *the* neighborhood in Maine where non-residents are most likely to receive a parking ticket.

Higgins Beach
Ocean Avenue, 207-730-4000
Latitude: 43.5621
Longitude: -70.2730

This 910-yard long beauty is considered "a private beach with public access." It's managed by the local Higgins Beach Association and the Town of Scarborough. The residents of this venerable neighborhood are very protective of their shorefront—there are just sixty-one parking spots for non-residents—so it's not the easiest beach to get on to. (You might want to leave your car in South Portland or Cape Elizabeth somewhere and bundle your beach balls and blankets into a taxi.) The beach has been a source of controversy between property owners and the public.

Sort of a shame, really, because this is truly a stunning stretch of coast, with sand that is fine and white and wide open to the rolling waves of the Atlantic. There's a cool old shipwreck (the *Howard W. Middleton*, which went aground in 1897), good kayaking, striper fishing on the Spurwink River, and great swimming due to the fact that the water temperatures here tend to be higher than at many other beaches, reaching into the 60s. And for a long time Higgins has been Maine's go-to place for surfers. This is a real, wide-open, stay-for-the-day sort of beach.

Follow Route 207 (Black Point Road), then turn left on Route 77 (Spurwink Road). Ocean Avenue is a side street of Spurwink Avenue. No fee is charged.

9

CAPE ELIZABETH

Crescent Beach State Park
66 Two Lights Road, 207-799-5871
Latitude: 43.5648
Longitude: -70.2281

Along with Scarborough, Crescent Beach is a go-to beach in the Portland area. Anyone in the Forest City looking for sand, sea, and surf generally ends up at one or the other. This mile-long stretch of white sand is just fifteen minutes from downtown—eight miles as the gull flies—and its neighbor is Two Lights State Park. All of which means it's a hopping spot.

Crescent Beach is a pocket beach in an inlet—Seal Cove—between two headlands, and its shape indeed matches its name. The southeastern part of Cape Elizabeth, where Two Lights is located, shelters the beach from the east, and Richmond Island has it covered from the south. So it isn't exposed much to the open sea and the surf is usually on the gentle side.

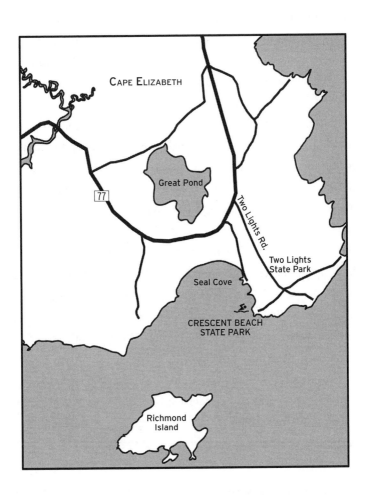

A barrier of grassy dunes separates the sand from a pine forest and these sandy ridges are busy with plovers and bedecked in beach roses in the high season. Rocks at the Two Lights end of the beach are fun to explore when the tide recedes. And the woods have a small network of trails connecting with nearby Kettle Cove State Park. It's all very pleasant.

All of the beach amenities are here, from the snack shop to the changing rooms, and lifeguards watch over the proceedings in summer. You'll see everything from hipster kids from SoPo, local couples holding hands, beach bums from the suburbs, to Midwestern tourists laying their eyes on the sea for the first time. The sand is beautiful and warm, ready for napping, and the sea is pretty perfect for swimming. There are picnic areas high up the beach in the grass. The beach is maintained in a natural state—it's not raked weekly in the summer like others in the area—which means you might actually see tidal wrack and seaweed. Some people are bothered by this, others like to peruse what the tide brought in.

Admission is $4.50 for adult Maine residents, $6.50 for non-residents, and $2 for seniors; kids under twelve are free. Parking lots can fill up in July and August so plan to be there early.

10

OTHER BEACHES IN SOUTHERN MAINE

Biddeford Pool Beach

Elphis Road, off Route 208, Biddeford, 207-284-9307
Latitude: 43.4428
Longitude: -70.3402

Nearly two miles long, on the ocean side of the lagoon known as Biddeford Pool, this beach is a wonder. The beach—and the Pool itself—were created by shifting sand flowing out of the Saco River. It's not the best address for a cottage—erosion remains a major issue and storms threaten houses—but it is a fantastic spot for swimming, surfing, and playing in the waves.

This is also one of the best birding destinations along the south coast. The open ocean, the lagoon, the marshes, the dunes—they all add up to prime habitat for our avian friends. So keep a keen eye.

Run by the City of Biddeford, the beach features lifeguards, restrooms, and public parking.

Fortunes Rocks Beach

Fortunes Rocks Road, Biddeford, 207-284-9307
Latitude: 43.4336
Longitude: -70.3712

Fortune's Rocks Beach faces the open sea from the east side of the finger that creates Biddeford Pool. At 3,740 feet, it is long and slender, with nothing to protect it from the full force of the Atlantic. Which means it's a great spot for surfers, boogie boarders, and anyone else who likes to play in the breakers.

The place takes its name not for those lucky enough to live here but from Francis Fortune, a Revolutionary War privateer who shipwrecked just offshore. Houses line the roads opposite the beach and parking is limited to permit holders (you can buy one at the town hall).

There are lifeguards and restrooms.

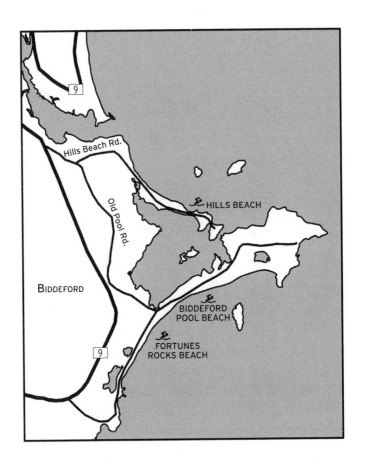

Hills Beach

145 Hills Beach Road, Biddeford
Latitude: 43.4545
Longitude: -70.3720

Hills Beach is both a neighborhood of two hundred homes in Biddeford and an actual beach in the epicenter of Maine beach culture. Unlike the Ogunquit, Wells, Kennebunk, Fortunes Rocks, and Old Orchard beaches all around it, Hills is somewhat quiet because access is limited. The sand is fine and the beach is very long and narrow, crowded by all those summer places. In spots there are grassy dunes. All told, there are probably five hundred yards of beach on which to spread out a blanket, but it sometimes feels as if all the eyes of Hills Beach residents are on you.

The Saco River slides into the sea just to the east of the beach. Combine that with the fact that Biddeford Pool backs up to Hills Beach like a grand lagoon, and add in the wetlands all along Newtown Road, and you have an ideal area for bird-watching. (Pick the right day, and you'll see a lot of people with binoculars around their necks.) All of the natural forces here combine to make the wave action less forceful than at other area beaches. The Biddeford Pool peninsula and a handful of islands—Wood, Stage, Negro, and Basket—protect it from a real battering. And in every direction, it seems, there's a lighthouse.

To reach the beach, drive right through the University of New England campus. Parking is practically nonexistent in the immediate area, so you may want to find a permissible spot at the school and hoof it. Likewise, there are no facilities or lifeguards, but there's also no fee.

Willard Beach

Beach Street, South Portland, 207-767-3201
Latitude: 43.6442
Longitude: -70.2276

Small and in a congested residential neighborhood, Willard Beach nonetheless attracts families to its compact, gravelly sand. The place is maintained by the local parks and rec department, which does a relatively good job, and the facilities include a concession area, outdoor showers, and a playground for young children.

What's most appealing about this four-acre park, though, is the look it gives you at Casco Bay: Fantastic views of Spring Point Ledge Light, several forts, and an armada of pleasure and working boats. You might even see a huge oil tanker on the way to the yard at Fore River, which will undoubtedly make you question the cleanliness of the water here (it actually does well in weekly tests). But as Maine beaches go, the temperature is relatively warm. Dogs are allowed between May and September, but only before 9 A.M. and after 7 P.M.

East End Beach

Eastern Promenade, Portland, 207-756-8275
Latitude: 43.6689
Longitude: -70.2408

This cul-de-sac is the only beach in the Forest City, and it's tiny, tucked underneath the Eastern Promenade. But the pebbly shore does share that boulevard's fine views out to the ever-changing wonders of Casco Bay. Islands, forts, lighthouses, boats big and small—you can take them all in. The beach is used more by dog walkers than by swimmers, but it does have a bathhouse and is a way of ingress and egress for the bay. (Portlanders also like to launch kayaks here.)

And it's a great excuse to wander over to Eastern Promenade Park, where you can connect with the Portland Trails network, fly kites, play tennis, or simply enjoy the vistas.

Drop down from Fort Allen Park to Cutter Street.

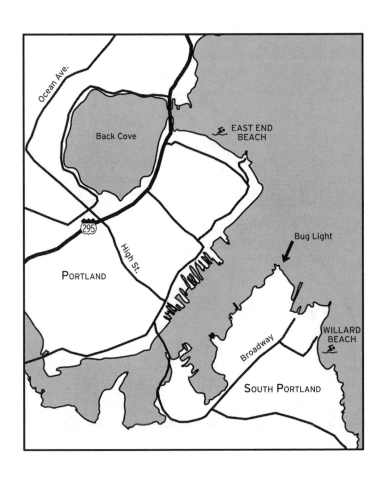

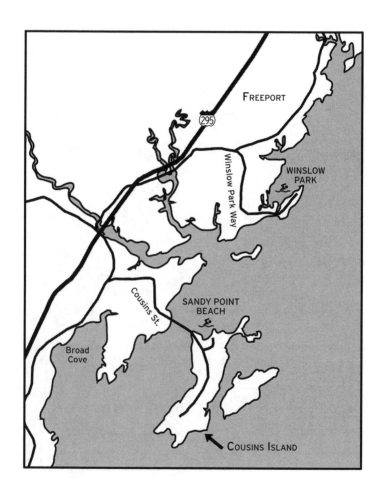

Sandy Point Beach
Cousins Island

An island beach? Won't that be hard to get to? Sandy Point is a beach on an island in Casco Bay, but Cousins is connected to Yarmouth by a bridge, so yes and no. This is a very petite beach—maybe more of a spit than a strand—on the north side of the island facing South Freeport. The beach is just over the Ellis C. Snodgrass Memorial Bridge (you might know it as the Cousins Island Bridge) from Yarmouth, and some of it wraps underneath the span. The sand at this former shipyard all but disappears at high tide. Not many people outside local residents know of the place. The parking lot can fill on a hot summer day, but the beach rarely seems excessively busy.

This is an exceptional put-in for anyone wanting to kayak Casco Bay. The swimming is good, and there's a lot to see and do—just realize it's small. Needless to say, there are no lifeguards or any sort of facilities.

The parking area is just over the Snodgrass Bridge on the left. No fee is charged.

Winslow Park

Staples Point Road, Freeport, 207-865-4198
Latitude: 43.8042
Longitude: -70.1128

If you consider the fact that L.L. Bean is one of Maine's largest tourist attractions, and that Freeport is a town known worldwide, it's amazing that this pocket beach, five miles from the Big Boot, is all but unknown. The tidal beach—best to get here two hours before or after high tide—is part of town-owned Winslow Park. As such, it offers visitors a lot more than simply swimming. The park's ninety acres include picnic spots large enough for family reunions, a play area for kids, a boat launch to get out onto the waves of Casco Bay, and even a nature trail that wanders along the Harraseeket River.

If you find all this to your liking, you can even camp here. There are 102 sites lined up along the bay. They're separated from the beach a bit, though, so it doesn't feel like the world's on top of you when you're spreading out your blanket. Swimming is excellent, but leave the beer and Frisbee at home—they're not allowed.

It's open from 8 A.M. to thirty minutes after sunset. The day-use fee is $3 per person, assuming you don't live in Freeport ($2 for residents).

11

PHIPPSBURG

Popham Beach State Park
10 Perkins Farm Lane, 207-389-1335
Latitude: 43.7468
Longitude: -69.7792

Set between the Kennebec and Morse rivers, Popham is by far the longest of the beaches in the Midcoast. The fine sand sprawls for more than three miles, and at low tide the beach is hundreds of feet wide. Surrounded by rocky shore for miles on either side, this beach is a geologic anomaly—one of the most welcome in all of Maine. The beach here is extraordinarily popular—a *Portland Press Herald* reader's poll had it ranked third in the entire state. Indeed, few other Maine beaches have all that it has to offer.

For years, Popham has led the line among Maine state parks—swapping the top spot back and forth with nearby Reid State Park—and often by a significant margin. As many as

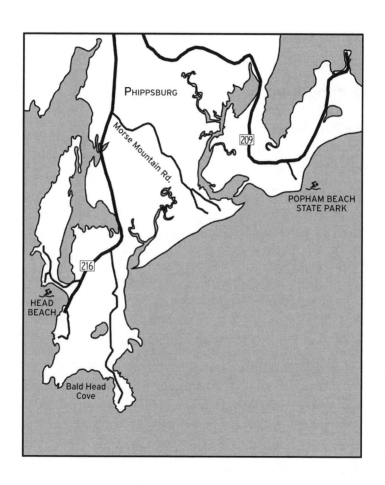

PHIPPSBURG

Morse Mountain Rd.

209

POPHAM BEACH
STATE PARK

216

HEAD
BEACH

Bald Head
Cove

180,000 people visit in a typical year, the vast majority in the eight or ten weeks of summer. On a hot day in August the cars fill the lots and spill out onto the road.

Popham hangs in the Atlantic at the end of the Phippsburg peninsula, a miniature cape jutting into the Kennebec River delta. At one end is that famous Maine waterway and at the other is the local Morse River. Between them is the long, shifting arc of sand. The length of the beach is one of its primary appeals—walk one direction and you can splash in deep channels cut by migrating water, walk the other and you can climb onto rocks and small isles. Unlike most beaches, which are just flat plains of sand, Popham is so complex there's days' worth of stuff to explore.

Most people, though, are simply content to stretch out on a towel or frolic in the breakers. And the beach is great for that, too. The sands are endless and warm and the wave action is fantastic for body surfing and swimming. Because of the cross-currents created by the flowing rivers, tidal action, and breaking waves, Popham is known for its undertows and riptides, so use caution. Lifeguards have your back.

Popham is also well known for its tide pools, its striper fishing, and its shell collecting. Clamming is popular here in the mudflats when the tide goes out (no license is required if you take a peck or less). The park's 529 acres include woodlands as well as beach, and along the edge of the spruce forest are picnic tables and grills. Just watch over your food—the seagulls are crafty and full of comical, often frustrating, ingenuity.

As a beach Popham holds its own against any others in Maine, and as a place to walk and explore it has few rivals. The views out to Seguin and Pond islands, with their lighthouses, are simply stunning. Those sites and others in the distance can keep you intrigued for hours, and the changing river corridor creates channels that can be deep and visually compelling right in front of you. There are headlands to climb, tide pools to explore, tidal wrack to pick through, and when the tide recedes you can cross the sandbar out to Fox Island, a tiny isle with still more vistas on which to feast your eyes. Just be sure to plan your escape and watch the incoming tide—people have been stranded here.

Intrepid hikers have been known to walk all the way to Fort Popham, too. The state historic site is three quarters of a mile up the Kennebec from the beach. Named for colonist George Popham, just like the beach, Fort Popham is set on a spit at the entrance to the river, and dates back to the Civil War era (construction started in 1861). Though it once had thirty-six cannon emplacements and slits for many more muskets, the place never saw action. Today, you'll find cool granite walls in a five-hundred-foot semicircle and great views.

History buffs will find plenty more to like here, too. Popham is the site of one of North America's earliest settlements, the Popham Colony, which was built not far from the fort. In August 1607, 120 colonists led by George Popham landed on the Kennebec just above the beach. They constructed a fort and a small village before suffering through a hard winter and being torn apart by infighting. Hoping to make it back to England before the cold came again, they cut wood and assembled the first ship ever built in America by Europeans—the *Virginia*. (Before leaving, they cooked up a great feast that some historians consider the real first Thanksgiving.) Every summer, archaeologists plumb the sands here searching for more clues to the Colonists' short-lived stay. (Or maybe they're just looking for a "message in a bottle," just like Kevin Costner, who filmed a movie of the same name here in 1999. Popham Beach stood in for North Carolina's Outer Banks.)

It's not just the early Colonists who have found the weather at Popham troubling. Hunnewell Beach at the eastern edge of Popham has experienced the greatest storm destruction of any beachfront in Maine, washing away in huge chunks during storms. The problems here have been so great that whole acres have disappeared, and the remaining beach has been drastically reduced in places—Popham is getting skinnier, putting a premium on the beach that's left. The effect has been so severe that the state has started issuing advisories whenever the high tide hits during peak visiting hours. That's when the water reaches so far up the beach there isn't much room for towels and blankets, making for an overcrowded experience. Park officials recommend planning your visit for an hour and a half on either side of high tide. The advisories occur four days each month, but can put as much of a damper on a beach vacation as days of rain, so call ahead. The good news is that a recent change of course for the Morse River promises a bigger beach eventually.

And when it arrives the people will be ready for it, just waiting with their towels.

Facilities include restrooms, a changing area, and freshwater showers, but you'll have to bring along your own food—there are no concessions.

The Popham Beach State Park Hotline (207-389-9125) has information on parking and tides and advisories. Fees are $4 for adult Maine residents, $6 for non-residents, and $2 for non-resident seniors. Kids 5–11 are $1. Kids under five and Maine residents over 65 are free.

OTHER BEACHES IN PHIPPSBURG

Head Beach

545 Small Point Road, 207-389-1666
Latitude: 43.7188
Longitude: -69.8509

On the same peninsula as Popham Beach, this strand is something of a local secret. It's part of the private Head Beach Campground and Cottages, but they allow non-campers to swim on its 325 yards of sand for a nominal fee ($5 to park). Set at the tip of the Phippsburg peninsula, the place is well worth the effort, with 300 acres staring out at Casco Bay.

Because it's private, the beach is nowhere near as busy as its state-park neighbor, and it's an entirely different experience. Gone are not only the crowds but the waves—Head Beach is protected on either end by ledges and doesn't have the big breakers that hit just up the road. The relative quiet and the gentle surf make it a great option for families.

Parking and restrooms are available and it's a short walk across the dunes to the action.

12

GEORGETOWN

Reid State Park

375 Seguinland Road, 207-371-2303
Latitude: 43.7901
Longitude: -69.7284

Every Maine beach has cold water, but Reid State Park has a reputation for being the coldest of all. We're talking all-over-ice-cream-headache type freezing. But that doesn't stop the crowds. This is one of the premier beaches on the Gulf of Maine and, like Popham, one of the rare stretches of fine sand in the midcoast. Which means it's one of the most popular places to be in the entire state on a sunny summer day. If it weren't for Reid, most visitors to Maine wouldn't have a clue where Georgetown is.

It's easy to understand the appeal. Reid is a beach-lover's beach—and the last big beach before the rocks take over. The sand here is soft and warm and stretches for more than a mile

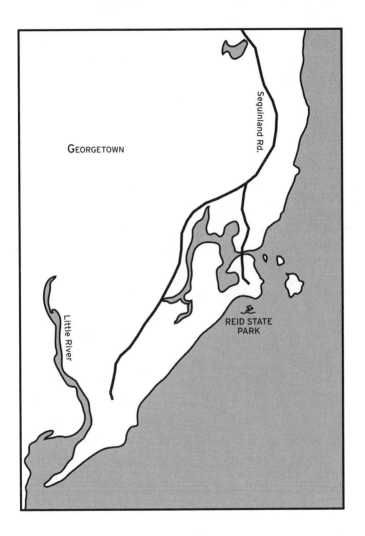

and a half between the Little River and Todd's Head. There are real breakers for bodysurfing—boogie boards, however, are not allowed. Plus, there's a shallow lagoon with its own beach where the water is probably twenty degrees warmer.

And there's more to Reid State Park than simply sand. That's what most people come for, but then they find themselves climbing up Griffith Head, the rocky overlook at the northern end, and staring out at the lighthouses on Seguin Island, the Cuckolds, and Hendricks Head. Or they wander down to the estuary at the southwestern edge. The park occupies more than seven hundred acres of varied terrain, from marsh to forest to rocks to riverfront to rare sand dunes. You could easily make a day here between traditional beach pursuits, hiking on the short network of trails, climbing on the rocks, picnicking at the tables and grills, and throwing a line out for stripers in the evening.

All this was donated to the people of Maine by financier and Georgetown resident Walter E. Reid in 1946, making it the first state-owned saltwater beach in Maine. Reid was director of Mack Trucks and owned a home just up the road from the beach (now the Mooring Bed and Breakfast). He loved the beach here and wanted to share.

The site has quite a colorful history. It was used for target practice by World War II pilots—buried ordinance was found here as late as the 1990s—and was the setting for another military training exercise in 1972. More than nine hundred marines set up here for Operation Snowy Beach during the winter, practicing extraction by sea. Locals sued to prevent environmental damage caused by the event, but the courts decided that almost a thousand soldiers, seven amphibious transports, several howitzers, and a handful of helicopters would have an "insignificant" impact. Newspaper reports said that the Soviets "shadowed" the U.S. Second Fleet during the maneuvers.

Today, the only things storming the beach are beachgoers and tiny piping plovers, which nest in the dunes (the dunes here are the northernmost sea grasses in Maine.) The plovers make comic runs to the water en masse, usually turning around to dart back out as the waves wash in, as if they, too, are afraid of the cold water. With the protections now afforded the cute little birds, it's hard to imagine any military exercises being allowed to happen these days. The dunes are periodically cordoned off to allow the birds privacy while they mate.

A whole range of wildlife can be spotted at Reid—or dug up. As at Popham, people like to search the sand for clams, usually near the mouth of the Little River. Seals occasionally pay visits, there are crabs and other critters under the kelp, and seabirds of all sorts can be seen. Striper fishing is also popular.

Rangers and lifeguards do patrol here and they keep the place in good order for both birds and bathers.

New bathhouses were built for changing a couple of years ago, and there is a full snack bar. Fees are $4.50 for Mainers over 12, $6.50 for non-residents, and $2 for non-resident seniors. Kids 5-11 are $1. Kids under five and Mainers over 65 are free.

13

BRISTOL

Pemaquid Beach

Snowball Hill Road, 207-677-2754
Latitude: 43.8712
Longitude: -69.5195

Sand gets increasingly rare the farther north and east you travel on the Maine coast. That's no secret. And it makes Pemaquid Beach, on the Pemaquid peninsula south of Damariscotta, something of a unique treasure. It's one of the last best places to find a long stretch of white sand in the midcoast; even so, it's nowhere near as packed on a hot summer day as the area's other rarified strands, Popham and Reid state parks. Another classic beach-lover's beach, Pemaquid boasts 575 yards of arcing white sand with all the amenities: changing rooms, showers, and snack bar.

The beach here is short and skinny compared to its cousins in the Bath area, fronting John's Bay and its picturesque islands.

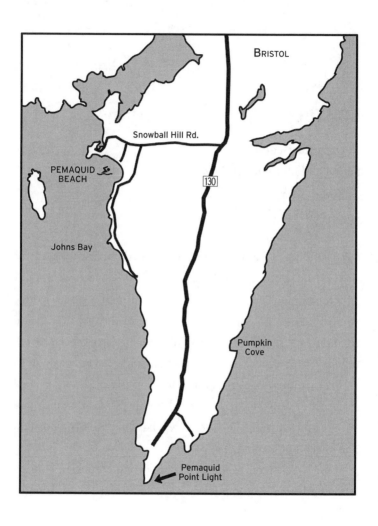

Because it faces west, it doesn't get the open ocean pounding that Reid does, and feels more like a harbor. (Leave the boards at home.) But the sand is soft and the swimming is great if you are of the warm-blooded sort—water temperatures are typically between 58 and 65 in the summer.

And the people sure do love it. Locals flock here like seagulls to french fries, and somehow visitors manage to sniff it out, too. Everyone in Lincoln County looking for a day at the beach puts in a day or a weekend or more here each summer. Some teenagers make it a daily habit.

Nobody appreciates Pemaquid Beach more than the Bristol Parks Commission, which also oversees the famous Pemaquid Point Light and a handful of other destinations. They manage the place and take great pride in it. Volunteers monitor water quality and protect the dunes, and the beach is consistently rated among the cleanest in the state by Maine's Healthy Beaches program.

In 2003, the Park's Commission joined with the Pemaquid Watershed Association to sponsor Beachcomber's Rest, a nature center right inside the beach pavilion. Exhibits and displays tell the story of this meeting place between sea and shore, and during the summer weekly touch-tank visits and interpretive beach walks, tide-pool explorations, art workshops, nature classes, and other events are offered. Sand castle competitions are popular, too.

For a small beach, Pemaquid has better amenities than many of the big boys. There's the usual snack bar with burgers and dogs and drinks (salads, too), and you can also rent beach chairs, umbrellas, and sand toys. The area's other attractions—Pemaquid Point Light, Fort William Henry, and Shaw's Fish and Lobster Wharf—are just a quick drive away.

The lot is huge, so there's generally good parking here. Day use is $4 per person for everyone over 12; kids eleven and under are free.

14

OWLS HEAD

Birch Point State Park

South Shore Road, 207-941-4014
Latitude: 44.0409
Longitude: -69.0931

Lucia Beach used to be something of a secret known only to locals and the occasional lucky visitor to Owls Head—which is surprising because it's a stretch of sand in the midcoast where such things are precious commodities. Tucked away on an anonymous side road, it was far enough from the main drag that most of the sweating masses on Route 1 never found it.

In 1999, this property was acquired by the State of Maine as part of the Land for Maine's Future Program and transformed into Birch Point State Park. Up went the sign indicating its existence to the motoring public. Yet it's remained surprisingly quiet.

When you pull up to the parking lot, and then walk the few feet onto the sand, it often seems there are more vehicles than

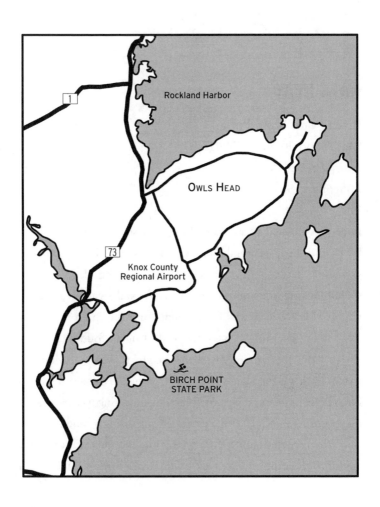

people to drive them. That's because a lot of the locals bring beach chairs and tuck them into the rocks and crags on the small headlands that wrap their arms around the pocket beach, preferring privacy to prime real estate. The sand is rather course anyway, but it's comfortable enough for a towel or blanket. And often it's all but yours.

The beach fronts the chilly waters of the Muscle Ridge Channel on the western edge of Penobscot Bay, and a few small islands dot the horizon. There is little wave action, so don't bother bringing the boogie board. Swimming is for the brave—this is cold water. There is some exceptional tide pooling to be done here, and kids love to climb the rocks and check out the woods that sit back invitingly behind them. A lot of visitors like to crawl along the interesting headlands or explore the cobbles that create a dune at the head of the strand.

While this is a beach in the state park system, it's no Scarborough, Reid, or Popham. There are a few picnic grills, some outhouses, and that's about it for facilities. There are no lifeguards to watch over you. And the $2-per-person fee is paid on the honor system in a small box. Open Memorial Day to Labor Day.

Still, the place is a small treasure. And the locals will wish you never found it.

15

LINCOLNVILLE

Lincolnville Beach
Route 1
Latitude: 44.2847
Longitude: -69.0075

Driving north on Route 1 after Camden, you can't miss this little beach. About 850 yards of grainy, tidal-wracked sand, it sits hard by the road. Across the street are a few shops and the local post office. Hemming in the beach to the north is the Lobster Pound Restaurant, a midcoast seafood institution. And immediately to the south is the state ferry to Islesboro, with its huge pier forming a literal wall at the end of the beach.

Like the small community that shares its name, Lincolnville Beach is ever busy on a summer day. Tourists passing by on their way to Acadia will slam on the brakes and hit the sand. Locals and people from nearby summer homes come daily and even

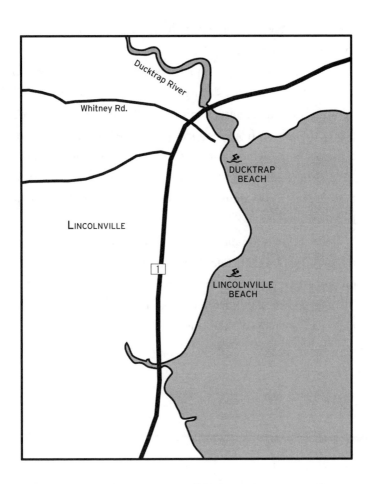

travelers waiting for the ferry will take a quick dip first—until this strand is hopping.

This is a swimmers' and gawkers' beach. There are no breakers big enough for surfing and the space constraints don't allow for much in the way of playing ball or jogging. But there's plenty to look at, from the faces of your fellow beachgoers to the faces in the windows of the Lobster Pound, and from the long, slender island of Islesboro that dominates the horizon to the state ferry loaded up with cars making its way there across Penobscot Bay.

The facilities are minimal, too. They put a few port-a-potties in the parking lot. And there are a handful of benches to sit on. Otherwise it's you and the beach.

The spot is a local secret so be respectful—and don't tell them where you heard about it.

OTHER BEACHES IN LINCOLNVILLE

Ducktrap Beach
Route 1
Latitude: 44.2965
Longitude: -69.0031

The real secret among beachgoers in Lincolnville, though, is not actually at Lincolnville Beach. It's just up the road where the pretty Ducktrap River, famous for its salmon, spills into the bay. Just off the last fire road before the bridge as you head north on Route 1 toward Belfast is Ducktrap Beach, where those in the know go. It's a diminutive peninsula that pushes out into the channel where the river emerges and the swimming is great on either side of this small point. Swimmers like to jump in on the Ducktrap side and ride the river's current out toward the bay. Just be careful.

It's a cobble beach with large stones, so leave your towel and blanket behind—bring a lawn chair and be respectful of the homes on the fire road that leads to the beach. There are no facilities and the parking is limited. No fee.

16

OTHER BEACHES IN THE MIDCOAST

Thomas Point Beach

Thomas Point Road, off Route 24, Cook's Corner, Brunswick, 207-725-6009

Latitude: 43.8945

Longitude: -69.8912

A private beach park on Thomas Bay, an inlet of the tidal New Meadows River—Thomas Point is better known for all the events it's hosted over the years. From the Maine Festival to its own bluegrass fest, the place has put on decades of shindigs and almost always has a full calendar.

And it has its own little beach. Two hundred ninety yards of sand, which grows increasingly rare as you head up the midcoast. The action here is at the whim of the tides, however, so you want to check the calendar if you intend to swim. There are lifeguards and the sands slope pleasingly to meet the lapping water and you can take a hot shower when you're done.

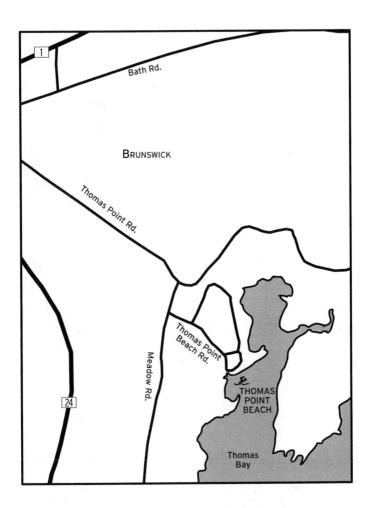

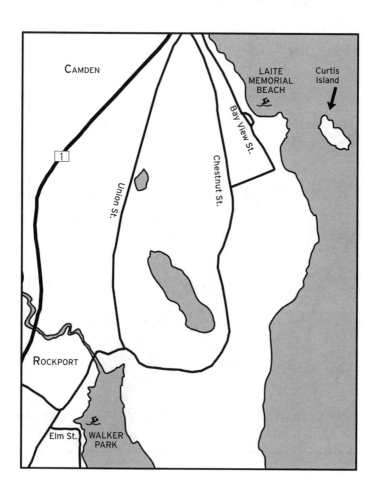

CAMDEN

LAITE MEMORIAL BEACH

Curtis Island

Bay View St.

Chestnut St.

1

Union St.

ROCKPORT

Elm St.

WALKER PARK

Otherwise, you can enjoy a host of activities, from simple picnics (choose from more than four hundred tables) to games in the pinball arcade. Kids love the big playground and the arcade, parents love the horseshoe pits and snack bar.

Admission is $3.50 for adults, $2 for seniors and children under 12, free for children under 3 and adults over 80.

Walker Park
Elm Street, Rockport
Latitude: 44.1823
Longitude: -69.0750

Known more for its swings and its merry-go-round, this small municipal park has a swath of actual beach at its feet. It's very tiny, but it has an outstanding view of Rockport Harbor, looking out at all the work and pleasure boats, the summer homes across the way, and the village on the hill. Just around the corner is another rockier stretch at the base of an old lime hill. The beach all but disappears when the tide comes in, so it's not the sort of beach where you set out a towel for the day. But it is a place to dip your toes in the water. Complete with parking, picnic facilities, and restrooms—and a pretty fine playground, too. No fee.

Laite Memorial Beach

Bay View Street, Camden
Latitude: 44.2040
Longitude: -69.0592

Part of Laite Memorial Beach Park, this tiny strand is another little-known gem. While the crowds flock downtown, those who more than to shop or dine drive up Bay View Street to this Camden Harbor park and its long, thin beach. Again, the sand is ephemeral—just a sliver remains at high tide—but this beach is nonetheless ideal for getting into the salt in Camden. Just like at Walker Park, this beach offers a fantastic view with your dip. The Camden Hills, the schooners in the harbor, an armada of sailboats can all be enjoyed as you swim. An offshore float waits a hundred feet from shore. Bring a blanket for the grass and a picnic hamper and make an afternoon of it. Kids can take to the swings; parents are usually content with the panorama.

There are restrooms and even an outdoor shower. Parking is limited but available. No fee.

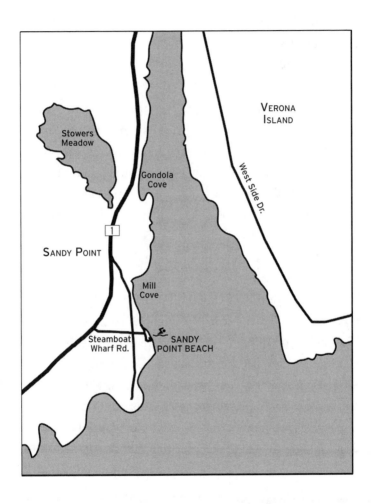

Sandy Point Beach

Steamboat Wharf Road, Stockton Springs, 207-567-3404

Latitude: 44.5695

Longitude: -68.7839

More than two million people every year motor to Acadia, many of them excited to visit gems like Sand Beach, the only large swath of sand in a national park famed for its rocky coastline. And on their way through Stockton Springs, these travelers drive past a wide-open beach that dwarfs Acadia's prized beach. Few people other than locals know that this Sandy Point Beach (not to be confused with the one on Cousins Island) exists, let alone that it's located within a half-mile of Route 1, tucked down a side street in Stockton Springs.

At 1,370 yards, the beach is big and broad, sitting at the point where the Penobscot River tumbles into Penobscot Bay. The sand is not the finest—kind of gravelly, really—and it gets a lot of tidal wrack. There are facilities—a seasonal, handicapped accessible public bathroom—and the beach itself has wheelchair accessible trails leading to the beach and a scenic overlook.

You'll find Sandy Point by taking the Steamboat Wharf Road straight though the intersection of Hersey Retreat Road. Steamboat dead-ends at the beach. Parking is not usually a problem, and there is no fee.

17

ELLSWORTH

Lamoine Beach Park
Route 184, 207-667-2242
Latitude: 44.4515
Longitude: -68.2856

Many of Maine's beaches have fine views—it comes with the
territory. But few offer sights quite like those at Lamoine Beach.
From its sand you look out at an astonishing panorama—the
mountains of Acadia National Park, all soaring and green.
Mount Desert Island is less than a mile away across Eastern
Bay. It's rather magnificent and, when you combine it with a
rare beach in the Down East region, it makes for a very appealing stop.

A lot of people confuse this little gem with nearby Lamoine
State Park. This beach is the centerpiece of the town-run Lamoine Beach Park. It sprawls for more than 2,740 yards—yes,
more than a mile of sand. Sand such as it is. Like many of the

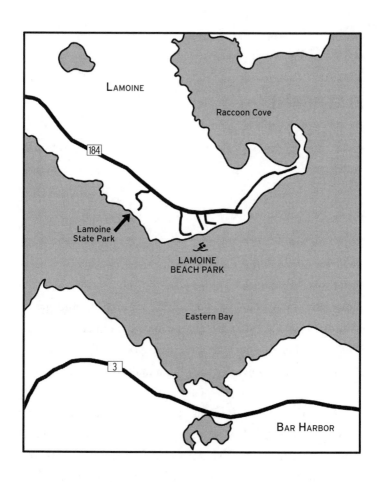

beaches of the eastern half of Maine, it's comprised of a small-grained, course gravel. It is fairly narrow, and the sand gets grittier the farther toward the water you go, but there's quite enough shore to go around.

The swimming is cold, as you can imagine, and the only surfing you'll do here is the wind kind. The facilities are limited to picnic tables and a boat ramp. It's a great place to launch a kayak for an exploration of Eastern Bay, and the wide grassy lawns that back up to the beach make for nice picnicking.

Many beachgoers will combine a visit here with one to the state park up the road, where there are bigger playgrounds, showers, and more picnicking spots—but no beach.

Take Route 184 off Route 1 in Ellsworth. Follow it for about nine miles. Go past the sign for Lamoine State Park, and within a mile you'll come to the parking lot for the beach. There is no fee.

18

BAR HARBOR

Sand Beach, Acadia

Park Loop Road, Acadia National Park, 207-288-3338
Latitude: 44.3292
Longitude: -68.1817

Sand Beach is a rarity—and not just because it's a beach of fine sand in the Down East province of rock. The sand here is composed of calcium carbonate—crushed shells. When you're running barefoot down to the water's edge, you're jogging over a cemetery of mussels, periwinkles, and sea urchins. Every beach has a certain amount of shell matter, but Sand Beach has the highest concentration north of Georgia—it's made up of almost 70 percent of the stuff. Makes the name of the beach a bit ironic.

A small pocket beach 290 yards long, Sand is not only one of the most popular in the entire state of Maine but also among the most picturesque. To the east is Great Head, at 145 feet, it's

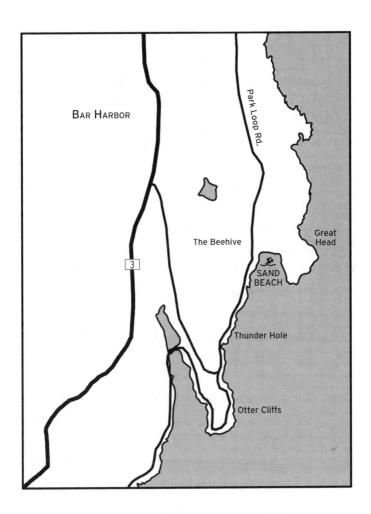

one of the highest headlands on the Atlantic Seaboard; and to the west is the Beehive, a craggy cliff face soaring up 520 feet (look closely and you can see climbers hugging the walls like so many bees). Out beyond the breakers directly in front of the sand is Old Soaker, a neat rock formation sticking up out of the sea, which has scuttled more than a few ships. And behind the beach is a marsh that beavers like to play in.

Because it's the only seafront beach in one of the nation's most-visited parks, sitting right off the main Acadia thorough-fare, Sand Beach is extraordinarily busy on hot summer days. The parking lot fills up early and stays that way for most of the day. This despite the fact that the water temperatures top out at about 55 degrees. Only the hardy dare swim here. (Kids tend to love it regardless, and there is no wave action to speak of, so they can have the run of the place.)

But there's so much to do even if you don't care to stick your toes in. You could scale either Great Head or the Beehive for another panoramic perspective on the beach. Or hit the aptly named Ocean Trail, a three-mile round trip that connects Sand Beach with Otter Cliffs, another of the park's most famous destinations. In between are all kinds of sites, from Thunder Hole to Monument Rock, that showcase the scenic seaside wonders for which Acadia has become known.

The human history of Sand Beach is almost as interesting as the natural. Many famous painters have set up easel here, from John Singer Sargent to Frederic Church (who gave the Beehive its name). New York financier J. P. Morgan gave the beach and the surrounding acreage to his daughter as a wedding present. And Spider Man has been known to frolic on these sands—well Tobey Maguire, the actor who played the web-slinger, has. He starred in *The Cider House Rules*, part of which was filmed right here.

Parking is always an issue at Sand Beach, so arrive early during the high season. There are places to change and restrooms are available. Free with the $20 park entrance fee.

19

ROQUE BLUFFS

Roque Bluffs State Park
145 Schoppee Point Road (Roque Bluffs Road), 207-255-3475
(summer), 207-941-4014 (all other times)
Latitude: 44.6084
Longitude: -67.4828

Like Lamoine, Roque Bluffs is unique among Maine beaches.
But not just because this 910-yard sand and pebble beach is a
rarity in granite country. It also offers the rare opportunity to
go for a dip in the frigid ocean and then step across the beach
and rinse off in the warm waters of a freshwater pond. Simpson
Pond, a sixty-acre freshwater lagoon, is just a skip from the
strand—sort of like taking a dip in the pool before relaxing in
the hot tub.

Roque Bluffs State Park occupies 274 acres on Schoppee
Point, a peninsula just south of Machias. The beach itself curves
for more than a half mile and it's a gravelly sand peppered with

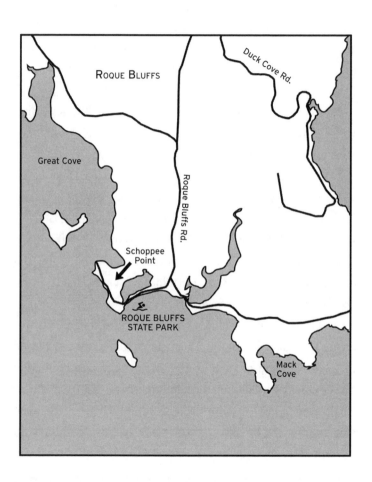

larger pebbles. Between the beach and the pond are picnic areas and a small playground for kids, and on the far side of the pond is a wooded area threaded with six miles of hiking trails. Bring your boots. And consider renting a kayak on Simpson Pond, too, it's a pleasant paddle and offers a neat perspective on the area.

Of course, wander too far inland and you'll quickly find yourself alone—everyone is here for the sand. This is not your fair-haired, beach bum sort of beach where you go to cruise chicks, hang ten, and shop for Ts. This is a much hardier beach where you'll look pretty funny in a thong, but you can swim and sunbathe, hike, fish, and launch a boat. Birdwatching is big as well. Much of the area around the pond is marshy, attracting a wealth of avian visitors. Eagles, sandpipers, plovers, gulls, and unusual species such as Barrow's goldeneye, Gadwall ducks, and hooded mergansers can be all be spotted.

Like so many of Maine's natural features, this beach was created by glacial activity. When the huge ice forms receded they left behind a moraine to the east of Schoppee Point, and the sand was washed here on the Englishman River. A raft of small islands just offshore protects the beach from the open sea, limiting the breakers. Those same islands, legend has it, were used as cover by pirate Samuel "Black Sam" Bellamy in

1717. It's said that he led a band of rogues here to hide, make repairs to their ships, and count their treasure. (Some say that's the origin of the name Roque Bluffs.) Bellamy even considered setting up a permanent settlement, a sort of retirement home for pirates, in this area.

The pirates liked what they found here, and so do the people of Maine. They voted in 1969 to preserve this beautiful spot as a state park. And they show their appreciation all summer long.

Take the Roque Bluffs Road from Route 1, then follow signs to Schoppee Point. The park is open May to October and there is a $3 fee for adults; $1 for children 5–11; and kids under 5 are free.

20

OTHER BEACHES DOWN EAST

Sandy River Beach
Off Route 187, Jonesport
Latitude: 44.5704
Longitude: -67.5713

Five football fields of beach in Jonesport? And no one knows about it? This stretch of sand on Chandler Bay way Down East is astonishing—not just because it exists but because outside of local residents, no one has made much noise about it. It's staggeringly beautiful, a long semilunar sweep of sand set before the islands and spruce-topped peninsulas for which Maine is famous. Dig in your toes and stare out at Roque Island. Go on the right day and it almost seems like you've stepped into the *Twilight Zone*.

But on hot days it's busy. There are no facilities and parking is limited.

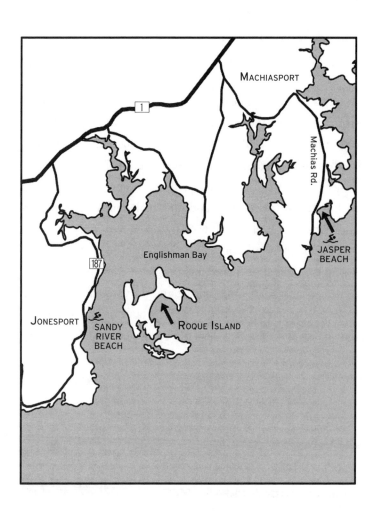

Jasper Beach

Off Machias Road, Machiasport
Latitude: 44.6273
Longitude: -67.3675

America's "foremost beach expert," Dr. Beach, calls this pebble strand the "Best Wilderness Beach in the Northeast." Whether or not he knows wilderness, he's not wrong that the eight hundred yards of singing stones here are special. The rocks are not jasper but a red stone called rhyolite—a fine-grained volcanic rock that polishes nicely—and they make enchanting clicking and clacking sounds as the waves wash in and out.

The beach protects a lagoon, and is backed by dense woods, giving it a wild atmosphere. Bald eagles are commonly spotted soaring overhead, the fog rolls in, and the views out to Howard Cove are majestic. A visit is more of an outdoor experience than a day at the beach—Jasper Beach is one of Maine's natural wonders.

Appendix: Beach Safety

(courtesy of Maine Healthy Beaches, for more information: mainehealthybeaches.org)

The Maine Healthy Beaches Program was established to ensure that Maine's saltwater beaches remain safe and clean. The program brings together communities to perform standardized monitoring of beach water quality, notifying the public if health risks are detected, and educating both residents and visitors on what can be done to help keep Maine's beaches healthy.

Summer in Maine means great times spent at the ocean, on the lake, or anywhere you might go to enjoy a swim. It's hard to imagine anyone would want to contaminate our beautiful natural waters with human or animal waste. But even though it's not deliberate, it happens. With a little planning, practicing healthy beach habits can be as easy as remembering your sunscreen.

General Hygiene: Healthy Habits
◆ Do not swim when you have diarrhea.
◆ Do not swallow the water.
◆ Shower with soap before swimming, and wash hands after using the toilet or changing diapers.
◆ Do not go swimming when an advisory is posted.
◆ Avoid water contact after heavy rainfall.
◆ Maintain and routinely pump out your septic system.
◆ Report any illicit or questionable discharges to your local plumbing inspector
◆ Properly dispose of pet waste and/or livestock manure.
◆ Maintain appropriate vegetative buffers along waterways.

Keeping Kids Clean

◆ Take your children for frequent bathroom breaks.

◆ Use "swim diapers" with absorbent padding.

◆ Change diapers frequently, away from the water's edge—in a bathroom if possible.

◆ Dispose of diapers properly. Place them in trash receptacles or seal them in a plastic bag to carry out with you.

◆ Wash your kid's hands when they've been in the bathroom. A sanitary wipe or liquid hand sanitizer can do the trick.

Beach-Loving Pets and Wildlife

◆ Scoop the poop. Carry it out or place securely in the trash. Keep an empty plastic bag tied to your dog's leash so you're always prepared.

◆ Check and obey the dog rules posted at your favorite beach or waterside park.

◆ Do not feed the birds or wildlife on or near the beach. Feeding can be harmful to waterfowl and water quality.

◆ Trash may attract waterfowl and other animals. Carry out all trash or dispose of it properly.

What kind of illnesses can someone get from contaminated beach water?

The most commonly reported symptom of water-related illnesses is diarrhea. Diarrheal illnesses can be caused by bacteria, parasites, and viruses such as *Cryptosporidium*, *Giardia*, *Shigella*, and *E. coli*. For more information about these bacteria and parasites, see cdc.gov/healthywater/swimming.

What are the symptoms of a water-related illness?

Vomiting, sinus infections, stomach ache, and other flu-like symptoms can be caused by contact with contaminated water. Other illnesses can include skin, ear, respiratory, eye, and wound infections.

How are water-related illnesses spread?

They may be spread by swallowing or having contact with contaminated water at lakes, rivers, or the ocean. The water can become contaminated by fecal matter, which carries harmful bacteria, parasites, and viruses. This unsanitary condition can be due to several possible causes:

◆ Improperly disposed of diapers
◆ Children not properly cleaned after using the bathroom
◆ Swimmers with diarrhea
◆ A vomiting or fecal accident in the water
◆ Wild and domestic animal waste
◆ Malfunctioning subsurface wastewater disposal or sanitary collection systems in the vicinity
◆ Nearby boats discharging sewage into the water
◆ Contaminated stormwater runoff

If you have a water-related illness
◆ Seek treatment from your medical provider.
◆ Report illness to lifeguard, beach manager, or staff on duty.
◆ To report the illness to the Maine CDC:
  207-287-8016/800-821-5821 or 207-287-4479 TTY
  disease.reporting@maine.gov

In addition to human pollution, beaches may be closed for a variety of natural reasons. Sharks and jellyfish have caused the closure of some southern Maine beaches in recent years. Algae blooms, such as red tide, can also cause closures.

Be sure to pay attention to any posted warnings about rip tides, and check the weather for storm activity out at sea. While the sun may be shining on the coast of Maine, a storm hundreds of miles away can cause rogue waves. Like rip tides, these are not to be taken lightly. People have been swept from the rocks at Acadia and other places on the coast.

The best advice, however, is to just use common sense. The most important thing is to have fun and just a little preparedness will ensure that you do.